**Chagall's
Moon**

# Chagall's
# Moon

Jeremy Robson

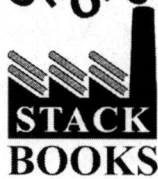

Smokestack Books 2023
1 Lake Terrace,
Grewelthorpe,
Ripon HG4 3BU

e-mail: info@smokestack-books.co.uk

www.smokestack-books.co.uk

Cover image:
David Abse,
Chagall's Moon

ISBN: 978-1-7391730-4-3

Smokestack Books
is represented
by Inpress Ltd

*for Carole,*
*who always cares.*

# By the same author

**Poetry**
*Poems for Jazz* (Leslie Weston Publications, 1963)
*Thirty Three Poems* (Sidgwick and Jackson, 1964)
*Poems Out of Israel* (Turret Books, 1970)
*In Focus* (Allison and Busby, 1970)
*Blues in the Park* (Smokestack Books, 2014)
*Subject Matters* (Smokestack Books, 2017)
*The Heartless Traffic* (Smokestack Books, 2020)

**Prose**
*Under Cover: A Poet's Life in Publishing* (Biteback, 2018)

**As Editor**
*The Young British Poets* (Chatto and Windus, 1971)
*Corgi Modern Poets in Focus* (Vols. 2 and 4, 1971)
*Poems from Poetry and Jazz in Concert* (Souvenir Press, 1972)
*Poetry Dimension 1* (Sphere Books, 1973)
*Farewell Performance: The Collected Later Poems of Vernon
    Scannell* (with Martin Reed, Smokestack Books, 2022)

# Contents

# Counting My Luck

I count my luck every day.
Whether waking early to rain
or a fiery sunrise, to frost or snow,
whether I'm waiting for clouds to clear
or sun to cheer, it's all the same,

I know that I'm the lucky one, seeing
the smile on your morning face as you
slowly descend the stairs towards me,
sleep still shading your eyes.

It's been like this for more years
than either of us can quite account for,
though if it would need a calculator to add
still more I'd dash out and buy one now.

But I know blessings can't be counted
and weighed like that. Best take things
as they come, whether they just add up
to one, or a hundred and one.

## Days of Awe

The days linger, the days race.
Is it real or is it virtual, this new life
we have to face? Friends call
from near from far to check we're
fine. A few we haven't spoken to
for quite some time. There's a special
camaraderie now, as in the war.

From our dugout behind closed doors
we wait the all-clear. We'll drink again,
but when, but where?

Our normally busy road is like an
empty village, the traffic tamed,
the few people that walk, walk warily,
except on Thursdays when we clap and
cheer, careful not to come too near.
The nightly TV briefings mostly tell us
what we don't want to hear.

No one wants to be a statistic,
to exit in that way. We take a welcome
evening stroll to clear the air.
Without a sound, my Samson hair
grows steadily towards the ground.

Friday after Friday evening the candles
flicker in the usual way, though sadly
there are candles of a different hue
we have to light to pay our due.
But the intimacy of a wedding joined
on Zoom moves us in an unexpected way.

In our garden, the birds are in full song.
Ever bolder, baby robins take careful steps
on tiny matchstick legs, peck peck at the
lawn as blackbirds swarm. We leave them bread,
watch them as they circle cautiously overhead.

We think of the Camps over which they say
no birds fly, and count our blessings every day.

# Turning Back the Clock

You can't turn back the clock, an old adage,
and yet today, as on previous end-of-October
Sundays, I did just that, or thought I had,
as scantily clad I crept round the house like
a thief in the still early morning while others
slept, climbing up on stools, stretching across
tables and windows to somehow reach
various old clocks and wind an hour back.

It seemed so simple, so imperious,
but all it really meant was that darkness
would envelop us that much sooner,
something I'd been trying to avert as
I watched what I ate, exercised daily,
walked myself into an exhausted state.

Of course I knew full well that in only six
months we'd be back where we were, or
some of us, the lucky ones, and everything
would be just as it was before as I turned
compliant metal hands forward once more.

Or not exactly so, as shakily and a little greyer,
I climbed back onto stools that seemed less stable
to reach clocks that appeared even higher than
hitherto, almost out of reach, while time itself
ignored the turning hands and continued at
its own steady pace as if in a never-ending race.

Who, I wonder, would I think I was kidding
as the ticking became ever more forbidding.

# Chagall's Moon

Such a welcome surprise, that sliver
of a seemingly electric new moon
hanging shyly between the rooftops
and chimneys of the houses opposite.

It had taken up its position early and
the sky on that balmy September evening
was still a rich unblemished blue. All it
needed then to make it a perfect painting
by Chagall were two young lovers floating
beneath the radiant banana-shaped moon,
a fiddler, a cow, and perhaps a hen.

But this wasn't Russia, or a shtetl scene.
No snow on the ground, no terrifying sound
of approaching Cossack horses, the lingering
smell of dwellings burning, the screams.

One by one the lights in neighbouring houses
were springing to life, and next door a television
too, clearly visible through the windows of a
ground floor room, a couple watching. It was
time, our watches told us, for the evening News.

In those anxious Covid days we watched, we zoomed,
so quickly turned from that innocent moon
to enter our own door and resume our nightly
encounter with the latest news and views.

No horses, no Cossacks, no blazing homes,
yet all around us, we knew, an invisible killer flew.

# No Longer Valid

With that pre-Brexit passport I'd be turned back
now for sure. Still, our decision to leave
the exclusive club we'd once signed up to.
One we yet may rue.

Anyway, I have a new passport now, not red but
a deep royal blue and no mention of the EU.
It's smart enough, my name place and date of birth
all OK, but with that wide-eyed, shady-looking photo
I could be taken for a criminal any day and still
brusquely turned away. Who can say?

Unsettling to think that were we plunged into another
major war we might end up on our own this time,
though some would say we were the last time round!
Ironic to recall who we fought against, and who we saved.

Seventy years on from that world war I vividly recall
celebrating the landmark date in a much bombed
village near the Normandy beaches where so many fell,
imbibing and raising our glasses with French friends, the
sky lit not by deadly rockets this time but by fireworks.
That heady night the entente was very cordiale.

Later we'd ambled through the narrow cobbled streets,
surprised to see large posters on all sides declaring
'Welcome to our Liberators'. Long torn down, I'll wager!

Now, as we join lengthy queues to cross European borders,
there'll be time to ponder as we find ourselves facing the
kind of stricture we've imposed on others, and still do.

But it's what we voted for and while £75 for a new passport
might seem extortionate, we're reminded daily of the fees
desperate refugees pay to cross our treacherous seas,
often battling through nightmare waves in flimsy dinghies
to reach a shore neither safe nor welcoming.

Clearly that price thought steep was extremely cheap.

# Counting the Cost

We follow the war's progress daily on
a mega-sized TV screen as if it were an
eagerly awaited game. Who's winning,
what's the score, who's been handed a
red card, what's been the night before?
It's obscene.

Meanwhile, bombs fall, rockets hurtle
at supersonic speed towards distant buildings:
homes, schools, hospitals reduced to rubble.

Desperate people, often old and frail, try
to leave besieged, collapsing cities,
others stay, and fight, and die,
though they exact an escalating price
as they boldly spin the dice.

It's murder on a massive scale, and
a cold-eyed killer won't desist, however
bloodied his nose, however hard they resist.

And we, for all our arms, can't stop him.
Like us, he too has weapons that could
destroy our world and might well use
them should we directly intervene,
and may do so anyway. He may not care.

We continue to watch the screen, and as
the images sink in it's hard to go about
one's own safe life as if it wasn't happening.

The umpire can call foul all he likes, and
has, but his whistle has no sound, and
the rules have long gone by the board.

How long will it last, when will the final
bomb be cast, the last person fall? Who
will finally call time, and at what cost?
Everything that's won is lost.

# When Stars Fell

That night, when stars decorated a clear
London sky and you drew close, you began
to hum an Ella and Louis number about an
unforgettably romantic night in Alabama
when stars fell on that once troubled state.

How different the histories of those two places
I thought, London with its kings and queens,
its palaces and regal parks masking its once
turbulent past when heads and bombs fell,
and Alabama, with its litany of racial bigotry,
the murders and beatings, the brutal policing,
the freedom marches Martin Luther King and
others led, the blood that was so freely shed.

And yet they still sang of heavenly love in that
hot southern state, those two jazz supremos,
as we did too on a rather cooler London night,
hoping those stars would not take fright.

# The Collector

My childhood passion, yet turning the pages
of those recently discovered old albums after
so many hidden years I hadn't expected this:
not all those historic faces from another era,
American generals and Presidents, Polish
aristocrats and Russian farmers, Egypt's
profligate King Farouk in his tasselled hat,
and, chillingly, a cold-eyed Hitler with row
upon row of Third Reich stamps lined up like
Panzer divisions behind him. G for Germany.

And how ironic to discover on the facing
F for France page, fatally placed, a down-cast
Pétain, caught in the glare of the Führer's stare,
looking across warily, as well he might, as if
about to leave the stage, his jaded Marshall's hat
perched precariously above a milk-white moustache.
Then, further on, Mussolini, Franco, Stalin and a grim cast
of history's villains waiting threateningly in the wings.

Surprising too, the regal faces of British Monarchs
on the stamps of countries that quit the Empire
long ago, so many of them, large and small.
And elsewhere too, striking stamps of proud nations
overcome by coups, revolutions, invasions, war,
now bearing different names or existing no more.

I must have spent all my pocket money
and many school-work hours I could ill afford
rushing to Stanley Gibbons in the Strand
in search of stamps I needed desperately
to complete a set, or to the post office to buy
First Day Covers and send myself postcards
to ensure they bore a day-of-issue postmark.

There they all are now, those stamps, neatly
spaced in sets or parts of sets and carefully mounted
or lightly held in place by small transparent hinges
on the appropriate pages; and those pretty First Day
Covers too, the 1948 Olympics, the Festival of Britain,
the Queen's Coronation, and also covers from a still young
United States with many centenaries to celebrate.

I wonder now at the care and time I took in those
early days, only too aware of my later slipshod ways.
Are they worth more now than the values they display?
For me they have a value far beyond the monetary.


## II


But there was more than that, for behind those
large long-lost blue albums others lurked, smaller
and more numerous, packed with the autographs of
the then famous – film and radio stars, dancers, singers,
sportsmen, politicians. I must have spent as much time
hunting them down as the stamps I sought, waiting
in the rain at stage doors, at the edge of tennis courts
and cricket pitches, outside football stadiums. And
for those beyond my immediate reach, there were
letters to send, stamped addressed envelopes enclosed
and a flattering fan note expressing my admiration.

It amazes me now how many responded in that
pre-email era, often with a specially signed photograph.
Were there more hours in those early days?
There must have been, for there were also cigarette cards
to collect, comics to hoard and sell on to eager friends,
amazing magic tricks to buy at Hamleys, and photos
to develop in the messy darkroom I'd fashioned
at the top of the house, the second-hand camera
I'd saved up for rarely rewarding my stamina.

# III

As well as all this I collected tropical fish, hurrying
as often as I could on a number 28 bus to an enticing
shop in the Harrow Road, where hundreds of exotic fish
of all shapes and colours swam and dazzled in tanks
around the walls. I'd press my eyes to the glass,
mesmerised, wanting them all, before selecting
one or two to take carefully home in a large jar.

Then, on one fateful birthday, I raced eagerly down
the stairs to find the hall floor flooded and the large
tank empty, all my beautiful fish dead. I tried to revive
them but it was too late. Not even my copious tears
could bring them back to life, nor the consoling words
of my mother as she mopped the floor. No killer,
no Lady Macbeth, could have felt more guilty.

My birthday party went ahead just the same
that afternoon, but I couldn't put out the candles
on the special cake my mother had baked, however
hard I blew. For me they'd taken on a different hue.

Somehow, after that, my enthusiasms waned,
the empty coffin-like aquarium was removed, the
stamp albums, the autograph books remaining exactly
as they were, last stamps, last signatures. Gradually,
unknowingly, I began to turn life's more transient pages,
as ever more swiftly I still do. Had that really been me?
Are all those books with their transporting pages mine?
Is it all true? It seems fanciful at this distance in time.

And yet, and yet... I don't regret.

# The Race

The others had quit the track, I had
no choice, I had to step up now.
It was like a fight. I grabbed the baton
in my shaking hand and clutched it tight.

I hadn't trained for this, and the race
was tough, circuit after circuit on rough
uneven ground. A jeering crowd was
cheering others on, and ruthless rivals
tried to trip me as I ran. It had been
like that since the moment I began.

It seemed endless – hurdles and streams
to clear, a winding course to steer, and
rising slopes that sucked the breath
as a raging wind tore into the overhanging
trees nearly bringing me to my knees.

I tried to preserve what energy I could.
Though it wasn't yet in sight, I sensed
the final lap couldn't be far away and
steeled myself for one last defiant dash,
determined to get there come what may.

There would, I knew, be no winning post,
just a finishing line, and once I reached it
I'd have to find the strength to raise the
baton high for another to nervously clutch
in his own reluctant hand while thunder
shook and lightning pierced the sky.

No time for sentiment or tear. He'd know
this was a race that could not be won, by him
or anyone. He'd also know his time had come.

# Meeting Picasso

I was supposed to meet Picasso.
I was given a time, but he wasn't there.
They told me he'd gone out to get some air,
to wait for him on the winding stair.

Eventually he came striding in, shook me by the hand
then turned to others in the ever-lengthening queue.
There was nothing I could say or do.

His assistant sauntered past, apologised, told
me to come again, same time, the following day.
She had multi-coloured ribbons in her fluorescent hair,
wore a long floral dress that swept the floor
and began to sing the Habanera aria from Carmen.
Not a woman you could easily ignore.

My Cubist dream continued through the night.
Now his paintings were hovering round my bed.
A man and an outstretched woman were entwined
in a passionate embrace, though things weren't
in their normal place. A bull was chasing a toreador
round a blood-stained ring, its horns half bent,
a guitar began to strum an out-of-tune lament.
I tried to fathom what it meant.

From the corner, an angular woman in blue
was eyeing me provocatively. I couldn't
place her though I thought I knew her face.
By now my head was spinning at a dizzying pace.

Still, I turned up next morning not a second
late for my important date with a book and
flowers I thought he might appreciate.
But they said they were sorry, he couldn't
see me as he'd just died. At least I'd tried.

# My Kingdom for a Muse

I've come to rely on mine, not just for
love, for subject matter, inspiration, to be
on tap to produce the sap when things
run dry, but to tell me when I'd banged
on too long, repeated myself, misspelled
a word, to cajole, console, convince me
lines are better than I think they are... or worse,
that a dash of humour does no harm,
always ready with comforting balm.

There were early candidates, perforce,
but they weren't the real thing, didn't
last the course, or perhaps it was me
who didn't. Surprising, though, what
anger, hurt and jealousy can do
to prompt a despairing verse or two.

It seems all struggling bards need their
own personal muse to help them through,
for there's no relying on nightingales to
fly by on cue and sing specially for you.

Did Shakespeare, I wonder, have such
a treasure standing over him, reminding
him that a sonnet had fourteen lines
not twelve, boning him up on all the
Kings and Queens he wrote about, all
the schemers, lovers, murderers, telling
him it was high time Hamlet made up
his mind, that Othello had lost the plot,
helping him to find the tricky rhymes.

With no Google, no dictionaries, no
thesauruses to turn to, he must have
needed several Muses by his side, have
been at it all the time given his output.
And think of all those others jostling to
come through, Donne, Herbert, Marvell,
Marlowe and the rest. Quite a queue.

And when eventually the lights went
down, the curtains closed and passion rose,
did they sign off, or was it then that their
real work began, part of the plan?

I certainly wouldn't have lent mine
to him or them, not for a moment, nor
to those who came later, the Baudelaires,
the Byrons, the Villons, the Dylans.
We all know what lechers poets are!

Besides, I need her here right now
to help me conjure up a closing rhyme.

She just wouldn't have had the time.

# A Spring Lament

Somehow, for all the turning years, spring always
surprises me, throwing off winter's chilling coat
often quite suddenly. And for the past few days
the almost unreal beauty of the blossom crowning
the branches of a young tree in the garden opposite
has stopped me in my tracks whenever I've passed.

But this morning, drawn by the disturbing roar of a
chainsaw, I peered through the window as a young
sun greeted the early day, and there it was, lying
like a corpse on the driveway, its pink finery scattering
as a steady wind began to lift its branches.

Nearby, three determined men sawed away at the
surrounding foliage, seemingly unaware of the dying
beauty at their feet. No execution, no falling guillotine
could have done more to dampen the spirits. I recalled
Hopkins' felled aspens, the poet's anger and lament.

The sun may have shone when those men began
their devil's work, highlighting the almost fairy-like
aura of the blossom on the ground, but now it had
been swallowed by thick dark clouds as thunder roared,
rain poured, and drop by drop the drenched blossom
lost its dazzle. The gods, it seemed, had spoken.

Next day it was as if it all had never been, a kind
of awful dream. Everything cleared away. I'd say
it was surreal, but sadly it was all too real.

# A Lovely Day

There I was on the morning bus, late,
lost in my own world, trying to arrange
evasive words on unfriendly paper, when
a high-pitched woman's voice cut in: 'Lovely
morning' she interjected turning towards me.

'Yes,' I muttered neutrally,
looking up then fixedly down, scrawling away.
'Not as hot as yesterday' she continued cheerily.
'Yesterday was terribly hot, and the day before'.

'Indeed' I responded coolly, turning away, not
wanting to engage, staring at the scribble on the page.

And so it went on all the way to town
until, realising I was well and truly beaten,
I put my notepad down, hoping I'd be able to
pick up the thread another, quieter day.

Reaching my stop, I smiled and slipped out quickly
as another man moved to take my seat.
His turn to face the heat.

'Such a lovely person I met on the bus today',
I thought I heard her bleat.

So wrong! She was old, she was grey,
all she'd wanted was a friendly chat to lift
her day, and I'd not managed even that.
Thinking back, I wondered what ghosts,
what nightmares, haunted her and
whether she was ever off the rack.

'What a bastard I met on the bus today'
is what I should have heard her say.

# The Cinema in my Head

No entrance fee, it's all completely free,
each night a different film, though not always
one I want to see. My own private cinema it might be
but the choice of film is never up to me.

Some are welcome, stirring warm memories of people
I've loved, people I've lost, but many are scary,
making little sense, with feared characters from
a long-buried past, or menacing strangers chasing
me down dark narrow alleys where mobsters lurked
or long-tailed monsters with flame-throwing eyes.
I pull the sheets over my head as I brace myself
to face the horror show ahead.

Occasionally, as I sleepwalk the next morning towards
the welcome day, I think back to the old Regal cinema
down our road and my youthful forays there. If you
were under fourteen and the film A rated, you had to be
accompanied by an adult, a law too risky to ignore.

So often I'd ask someone in the queue to take me in.
Strangers they might have been, but it felt completely
safe in those innocent days and few refused.

Now, though my loved one lies close in those deep
hours when our worlds are separated by sleep,
I feel far from safe as I clutch the sides of my bed
and brace myself to face the images in my head.

# An Evening Drink

That stupefyingly hot evening we were relaxing
in the shade, two large Martinis in our hands,
when a collapsed deckchair caught our eyes.

We'd already spent too much time that afternoon
trying to repair it, struggling with parts that didn't
seem to belong anywhere, but for some reason
we put our drinks down and decided to try again.
Not for long though, as tempers flared in the mind-dulling
heat that seemed to us like a desert *khamsin*.

Defeated, we returned to our drinks and chairs
that were solid enough, but behind our backs
a family of wasps had inhabited our Martinis.
When, disconsolately, we tipped them out,
they appeared to be dancing round the lawn.
They couldn't have drunk that much, but perhaps
they weren't the boozers I'd taken them to be.

That, I realised, was the end or our evening drink,
as I poured what was left of it into the sink.

# A Beethoven Fantasy

Beethoven was his passion.
Often in the early evening when
a blue mood overwhelmed him, he'd
lie back in an armchair, a large malt
whisky by his side, immersing himself
in the great quartets and sonatas.

Or sometimes, in a more up-beat mood,
he'd nod, conduct and sing along as
a symphony soared to its cathartic climax.
He knew every note, every mood change,
every stirring melody. And it had been that
way for several years now since, his hearing
fading, he'd bought himself a pair of costly
aids for his sixtieth birthday.

They had transformed his life, enabling him
to tune in to the music he loved, but also
to the morning song of the cuckoos in the
distant trees beyond his bedroom window.
Often too, rising at dawn, he'd follow a favourite
route through the still misty woods, enjoying
a special kind of concert as waking birds
regaled him with their flute-like solos.

One winter night a sudden thought excited him.
Supposing, as he became deafer, Beethoven had
been supplied with a modern aid instead of the
ineffectual crude contraptions he'd often tried.
How different might everything he wrote in
his later years have been? What else would
he have written, would the range, key, and timbre
of his work have been transformed as other
sounds entered his musical vocabulary, as his
tortured life took on new harmonies? What arias
of love might he have blessed us with?

He smiled at the thought, put down his glass, and turned another page of the Beethoven biography he'd been immersed in. Was it true, he asked himself, that the great composer had died during a thunderstorm? He tried to imagine what Beethoven would have made of that, had he been able to, and in what dramatic form. The symbols clashing, the brass section at full blast, the bass drums rumbling ominously.

He paused, put on his favourite symphony, turned the volume up a notch and poured himself another scotch.

# Just Passing By

I wasn't spying nor even prying, but the lights
in their front room were ablaze and seized my gaze
as I passed absentmindedly on my evening stroll.
It was in blinding contrast to the surrounding houses,
most of which had their curtains fully drawn.

A woman in a bright red jumper, her back to me,
was playing an upright piano fervently, her hands
racing across the keys, her head moving from side
to side. It was like a stage set as she sat there
in the spotlight amidst the falling night.

I couldn't quite hear what she was playing nor
see her face, but there was a portrait on the wall
at the back I felt sure was of her. A smiling
attractive young women with blonde hair
and striking eyes, looking slightly surprised.

Books and papers were scattered everywhere
and there were other paintings hanging between
the shelves which I couldn't clearly see. As she
paused and sipped a drink I wanted to applaud, but
instead stepped back under the cover of a nearby tree.

Then suddenly, from somewhere, an uncomfortable
childhood memory surfaced of my own weekly encounters
with a not always patient and by no means young piano
teacher with a strong middle-European accent, and of her
scratched upright piano at the back of a dusty room.

She'd sit beside me beating time with a ruler that only just
missed my hands and almost sent flying the mysterious
sheets of music I was trying to decipher. However hard
I tried I could never get it right.

Sometimes in summer she left the window slightly open,
and arriving early, I'd wait outside enjoying the passionate
music that flowed from the piano within. But when she saw
me she'd stop immediately. Teaching ungrateful pupils like
me must have been, for her, a necessary nightmare, and I
often wondered what had happened to her own career.

Clearly, for me, the piano was something to listen to
not to play and we soon went our separate ways.
A Brendel or a Rubenstein I would never be.

As my mind and focus returned to the present and
the captivating scene before me, I watched a tall handsome
man enter carrying two glasses that seemed to be filled to the
brink. She paused, turned towards him, smiled, took one of
the glasses and raised it high. I could almost hear them clink.

Then they held hands, the lights went down and they slowly
left the room, leaving me in the enclosing dark to imagine
the next off-stage, censored, passionate scene... and continue
my solitary walk as if what I'd seen had never been.

## That Stormy Night

'The Gods must be crying tonight,' she murmured
as a ferocious baying wind continued to pound our
house, rattling the windowpanes, bending tall trees
to the ground, making floorboards creek. There
seemed to be something spooky on the prowl, and
as the pitch-black night closed in over our bed she
edged ever closer and tightly gripped my hand.
The wind continued to howl like an unruly band.

Eventually she sang herself to sleep, a kind of blues
that hung in the air, coming from I knew not where,
a slow, haunting melody I didn't recognise that
continued to revolve around my head as morning's
welcome light crept in, and slowly and gradually she
moved safely away across the crumpled bed.

# Gone Away

*remembering Dannie and Joan Abse*

That house was theirs, it always will be,
so much mirth, joy, pain, so much patient
work — she an art historian, he a poet —
many vaunted books between them,
and children whose laughter echoed
down the stairs in their early years.

But after they'd died others came, as others
will, and began to change it all, as others do,
not knowing into whose lives they stepped.

Yet in my mind anyway it remains exactly
as it always was, the piles of letters and
notebooks on the old oak desk, books
and journals overflowing the shelves,
and, side by side, two deep-sagging armchairs
facing the old TV in the small front room.
So many dramas, sporting encounters.

Driving past, as we frequently do, we've
watched as strangers altered that house,
a tarmacked drive replacing the hedge
and small front lawn, the door a bright
sparkling blue, the stucco on the walls
repaired and now a gleaming white.

Have they changed the informal garden
at the back, I wonder, thinking of the old
cooking apple tree they'd sit under when
summer blazed, reading and talking.

One day a blue plaque will doubtless record
their long sojourn there, two special people's
lives in a formal word or two. It just won't do.

# Calling Cold

No, I'm not the person you want,
and if I am I'm not in now!
I don't believe you plucked my
number from the air, I'm not fool
enough to fall for your serpentine guile.
You're so obvious I can almost see your smile.

Insist in that silky voice all you will, but I
don't and won't believe you're calling from the bank,
that my computer's about to blank, my phone
to be cut off, that the tax man's at the door.
Please don't persist.

I feel blood rushing to my head.
How dare he raise me from my bed.

No, I'm out, I'm away, not coming back.
Remember that next time you try to hack.

# On My Way

Strolling up Camden High Street yesterday,
minding my own business, my eyes locked on
the flower stall at the corner where a man was
filling a large wreath with fresh white carnations.

Returning a little later I saw he'd filled
another six, each now displaying a different
letter of a woman's name, the same as that
of someone dear to me, a haunting vision
which shocked and made me shiver.
Though the day was bright, the letters screamed
at me like searchlights in the night.

Not a Jewish funeral this time round perhaps,
and so no Shiva, but death was not the place for division,
I told myself, and grief has no religion.

Deep in thought I walked towards the station,
surprised to see a silver kiddush cup sparkling in
the window of a charity shop I often stopped at.
The family silver it might once have been but clearly
someone had gone and it had been handed on.
God knows how many Friday nights it had seen,
the family assembled, the candles lit, the wine
sipped, challah bread cut, the Shabbat ritual.

It seemed so forlorn I thought of rescuing it
and taking it home, but death it seemed was
stalking me that day. So I pulled my mask up high,
turned abruptly and hurried on my way.

# The Night that Was

That locked-down Passover we could
expect no Elijah, not even a virtual one,
the door firmly shut, though the family's old
silver wine cup, filled to the brim, still awaited him,
as it had the year before and over many
joyous years, welcoming. You never knew.

The normally crowded table
was set for two.

Yet we celebrated as best we could,
zooming and skyping as many would,
a Passover service like no other.

'Next year in Jerusalem' is what we say
'Next year anywhere' is what we pray.
The songs we sang were in a minor key.

'Why is this night different from all other nights?'
the family's youngest normally asks.
Why indeed?

That Seder night there were even more
than the usual questions, and fewer answers,
more to contemplate than the unleavened bread,
the bitter herbs, and the Exodus story we read.

The ten gruesome plagues God visited
on the Egyptians were all too real that night
as thousands round the world still fell
to an invisible one every bit as cruel.

The drops of wine we spilled, one by one,
as each of those plagues was recalled
seemed to have become more like real blood
than the blood they symbolised.

That we should be continuing to suffer
one ourselves while extolling others
might be history's irony.
Was God's hand in this?

Let our people go, but let all people live.
Now was the time to reconcile and forgive.

# A Seaside Photo

Aged five, splashing in the sea and
watching seagulls dive, there was
not a cloud in view that August day,
the endless sky an undiluted blue.

And time, if he was aware of time, was not
a chiming clock that beat the hours down,
but his mother's call to high-tea, a story
read together on the old settee, and bed.

And there to dream of white-foamed waves
and sandcastles, of crabs scuttling across white
sands, of pony rides and Punch and Judy shows,
of the billowing sails of colourful yachts, and
of the elegant pier that seemed to stretch to the
horizon, where bands played and you could shy
wooden balls at coconuts that never seemed to fall,
have your fortune told, and wolf candy floss,
waffles and ice-cream to your heart's content.

A few years later and he'd be standing at the
edge of the Great Orme cliffs, throwing stones
at transparent jellyfish below in revenge for
swelling stings that had made him scream.
Now smugglers and pirates filled his dreams.

And so it went on, the annual visits to his
great-grand-parents' Llandudno home where
he was born, while the oblivious tide rolled in
and out with military precision and the sea raged
and calmed, calmed and raged, those idyllic
summers rolling him steadily towards adult
hurdles more challenging than breaking waves.

Yet he returned there from time to time, if only in his dreams, and once, proudly, with his wife and young family, but the endless summer days he vividly recalled seemed to have become much shorter, the sea more often rough than calm, and there were too many disturbing ghosts around.

# After Hours

Those after school hours were the ones
we relished, no rules to break, no strict
spoil-sport masters lurking round corners
to haul us in for some trivial sin.

In winter I'd race home, keen to get my
homework out of the way so the BBC's
addictive Dick Barton radio thriller could
hold sway, as it did in millions of households
throughout the land five nights a week.

I never missed it, and at six forty-five I'd be
pressing my eager ear to our melanite set
in the kitchen as thrill followed thrill, leaving
listeners in suspense as the closing music
galloped towards its heart-pounding climax.
Would our Special Agent escape this time?
Night after night I was there, waiting on
tenterhooks for the next instalment to air.

That, and the latest Biggles book was what I'd
kill for. Those books, with their faded bluish
covers, still take pride of place on our living
room shelf alongside Henty's racy historical
adventures. They remain personal mementoes
of something I can't quite define, uniquely mine.

Lengthy summer evenings gave more scope:
to practise batting and bowling in the nets,
to rally on the tennis courts in the local park,
to volley against the side wall of our house
which I'd do for hours until night fell, practising,
forever trying to become more skilled, my
dreams of Wimbledon never fulfilled.

Girls were not yet on the scene, or not quite,
their mysteries still locked away for a later day.
How amazingly innocent we all were then, but
once the apple was bitten nothing would ever
be the same, the game quite different with
more complicated rules, not always fair, not
readily understood. And however hard I'd try,
I'd not always find it easy to comply.

## That Summer Night

Her lips were warm that sultry
summer night as we canoodled
behind the old club house, well
out of sight of the revellers within.

It meant the world to me
that first lingering explosive kiss.
'I wouldn't do this if I didn't love you',
she whispered quietly, and 'this' was simply that.
Just thinking of it brought colour to my cheeks.
I didn't wash my lips for weeks.

There were later teenage forays, ever
more adventurous, but that first innocent night
was the one that mattered most, though the others
were the ones about which I'd loudly boast.

# Jazz in the Night

I came to cherish those restless nights when sleep
turned its back on me, and those intimate moments
I'd share with the old jazz masters as choosing a disc I'd spin
it on a turntable almost as old as the recordings themselves.

Louis Armstrong's Hot Five was usually favourite, scratched
and crackling though it was. Its exuberance and stomping
rhythm seemed to relieve my up-tight mind more than
the dazzling pyrotechnics of the greats that followed them.

They brought an era to life, though it was sometimes at funerals
that their music was played. Listening to them it was impossible
not to tap your feet, to resist the glory of trombonist Kid Ory,
the driving piano of Armstrong's wife Lil, the heaven-sent
high notes of Louis himself, or the vibrant clarinet of Jonny
Dodds. It was enough to placate any listening Gods.

The verve, the passion, the roughness of it all was
its special appeal. This was art in the raw and I loved it
and all the richly-named numbers they played –
Strutting with some Barbecue, Muskrat Ramble, Irish
Black Bottom, Yes! I'm in the Barrel, and Heebie
Jeebies were among my many colourful favourites.

Gone they might be those early Hot years, yet for me
they lived on in the old spinning discs I listened to while
darkness reigned, swaying and singing until morning tamed.

# In an English Garden

She seems so at home, lying back, eyes
half-closed in her comfortable deck chair,
the sun spotlighting her hair, a book spread
open on her lap, so much part of the landscape,
so at ease amidst the roses and dahlias,
the hollyhock and lavender, the apple trees,
the mauve and white lobelia trailing down
the sides of the old wooden tubs.

A perfect English scene perhaps, but not one
she could ever have envisaged when, as a
young girl, she ran to school each carefree
morning along the Nile, the sun scalding the
dusty streets, the swaying palm trees and
the delicate scent of jasmine ever present.

Often she'd recall how she lingered at the busy
kerb-side stalls, wistfully eyeing the tempting piles
of almonds and pistachios, the colourful plates of
dates and figs, the watermelons and mangoes,
as lizards darted for cover in the nearby rocks.

Is that what she's day-dreaming of now I wonder
as I, her English husband, watch silently from an
upstairs window, and in what language?
Or is it of the long summers on the beaches
of Alexandria, or her parents' makeshift chalet
in the desert near the Pyramids of Giza, the
whirling sand that always filled her hair and
the exciting birthday parties she'd enjoyed there?

Occasionally she frowns, as if less pleasant memories have suddenly overtaken her, then suddenly she stirs, and as her eyes open and she focusses on the jigsaw-shaped white clouds of an English sky, she turns. Could it have been the robin perched boldly on the arm of her deckchair like something out of a Christmas card that disturbed her reverie? She smiles, and maybe it's thoughts of her own young family that absorb her now. Impossible to enter other people's dreams, their secret lives, however much you may endeavour to.

Rising slowly, she walks thoughtfully across the smoothly cut lawn of her English garden towards the safety of the home that has become her own.

# Old Friends

As always I arrived too late.
They'd long gone, and all I could do was
stare at the posters and photos that line
Deauville's long beach-side promenade,
absorbing their presence and fantasising...

...of saying Bonjour to Françoise Sagan,
whose Tristesse was part of my own departed
youth, and who liked to spend the late
summer there when the crowds had left,
thinking, dreaming...

...or of telling an affable Simenon, who'd come
in his boat to sign books in the sea-front Café
du Soleil, that Maigret had lost the plot...

...or of peering over Fernand Léger's
shoulder as he absorbed the kaleidoscopic
colours of the old-fashioned parasols on
the beach and painted them abstractedly.

But above all its to the Sagan poster I regularly
return, with its photo of a lovely be-jeaned girl,
stretched out on the empty sands, book in hand,
her words beneath, with their simple beauty all
the more poignant for the subsequent turbulent
life she was to leave too early in nearby Honfleur.
*'Je regardais la mer vide... Rendue à la solitude,
à l'adolescence rêveuse, à ce qu'on ne devrait
jamais quitter'.*

Would those habitués of the once fashionable
resort have bridled at the thonged, topless lovelies
that spread themselves on the sands these days?
Hardly! I recall an early Jean Gabin film in which,
looking down as he embraced an old flame, the
actor exclaimed, 'Nice to see old friends!'

They may have departed, and the great artistes too
who'd performed there in the glitzy casino where
fortunes were gambled nightly on the spin of a wheel,
but the same sea still spills its waves onto sands
that seem to stretch for ever, and the show-off pigeons
still loop the loop as we cautiously approach, many
years too late perhaps but still imbibing it.

It's nice to see old friends!

# Last Writes

I've been waiting all my life for this,
but if that's the best they can do I'm
not at all sure I want to follow through.

Those elegiac words can't be for me.
They don't know the half of it! I've been
editing other people's words all my life
but now I can't remove so much as a comma
or add some spice. They must be joking!
They need my advice.

It's a strange-shaped box they've put me in.
They've totally misjudged my shape and height.
Can't they get anything right? And those po-faced
men in black, and the others loitering at the back,
leaning on their shovels. I don't like the look of that.
If this is a dummy run it's not much fun

Someone is droning away in English.
A rabbi? Call that a rabbi? An old Jewish joke
starts to surface in my mind. Not I suppose the
time or place, though it might wipe the gloom
off everyone's face. I need more space.

The venerable rabbis I recall from the endless
services I endured during my compliant youth
had long grey beards and prayed in Hebrew, which
made more sense, even if I didn't understand
a word. It's my moment now and I want the real thing.
I demand to be heard or I'll make a scene.

Smiling to myself I remember the epitaph
the irrepressible Spike Milligan wanted on his
headstone. 'I demand a second opinion.'
You have to laugh.

Now something is dropping on the lid of the box,
mud I presume, and those shovels at work at last.
What a din! Can't I rest in peace? Is that a sin?
I fear it's going to become hard to breathe.
Soon time I guess to test those theories about
an after-life or resurrection, or even, God forbid,
about Hell. Much more of this and I'll start to yell.

Anyway this farce has gone on long enough.
All quite an anti-climax really after such a build-up
over the years. I need company, I need laughter,
lively good-looking women and a bottle or two
of the finest Scotch. Yet you want me to lie here
snoring my head off for eternity. It's so boring!

I'm climbing out now.
I'm glad you've woken me. Not a dream I've
enjoyed, not for a moment, far too real.

Thank the Lord it wasn't the real deal.

# A Secret Cure

With his agonising stammer the new
boy was an easy prey for the foul-mouthed
bullies in our raucous fifth-form class.
How they relished the long silences that
echoed when an insensitive master
hurled an awkward question at him.
Worse still were the French orals when
his words came slowly, bit by it, or not at all.
They couldn't wait to see him stall.
That he was clever seemed to make it worse.
It was an additional kind of curse.

Those tense shameful moments, when
I'd sat at the back of the class biting my
normally lively tongue, came back to me
vividly long after when, one evening, I
spotted him entering the underground
carriage I was in and as I looked up from
my paper we caught each other's eye.
We began to talk, his speech now strikingly
fluent. I couldn't help wondering why.

It took a while, but after we'd met again
and enjoyed a drink or two, he began to tell me
how a skilled physician had hypnotised him
regressing him back through his childhood,
year by year, until he'd found the cause.
He never told me what it was and I didn't pry.

Gradually, under that doctor's sensitive care,
his stammer had vanished and his words
had begun to flow, the trauma overcome.
A battle won.

Years later, when my doctor father died,
on reading through the files of letters
grateful patients had sent him, I discovered
the young boy's secret for myself, for he'd
been my father's patient, and there, in his
own young hand, was his own disturbing
yet ultimately triumphant story.

Although reading it gave me a kind of guilty thrill,
it was a confidence I knew I shouldn't have
intruded on, one I've kept and always will.

# The Way of Things

I've seen too many of those close to me
depart this earth with all the black
ceremony death imposes when a life closes.
I'd counted on them being here forever, yet
know too well that's not the way of things.

And daily too I've shared in print the lives
of people I never knew, marvelling at what
they'd brought to the world they'd left, often
without fanfare or the praise that was their due.
How quickly they pass into history.

But I've also watched in wonder as two very
dear to us entered our world, enriching our lives
as they grew towards adulthood, shaping their own,
laughter and celebrations filling our home.

These days the seasons seem to turn with
accelerating speed as we observe the shrivelling
leaves give way to autumn winds, then begin
to grow again as the cold recedes, days lengthen,
and we wait to see what surprises Spring will bring.

And always it reminds us that there's as much
to hope for as to regret, that it's this birth
and re-birth that disperses life's darker scenes,
even as we strive to divine what it all means.

# Old Cuttings

I've been sorting old cuttings from way back
about someone with my name, though I can't
believe that he and I are one and the same.

Trimming the well-delineated edges of the
pages piled up on the kitchen table, I realise I've
never seemed able to cut in a straight line, a fitting
reflection, I'd say, of a life that has never gone
in a straight line, forever driven as it's been
by unexpected detours and encounters.

Why, I wonder, do I always appear to have
followed the longest route from A to Z, caught
the slowest trains, taken endless wrong turnings,
always late however important the date.

Not surprisingly Sat Navs have never worked
for me. Alarmingly, the last time I tried one,
lost as I was on a misty night in a country lane,
a woman's voice kept commanding me to turn
left, turn left, and slavishly I did, screeching to
a halt just feet from the bank of a fast-flowing
river. Reversing, I beat a hasty retreat, and did
for her as quickly as she almost did for me!

Dangerous to follow other people's voices is what
I learnt from that escapade, though I was lucky later
to have found one that has always turned me in the
right direction whenever I was in need of correction.

Now here I am, on a dark rainy day, snip snipping
the edges of yellowing pages – for what purpose,
I wonder, laying out these transient moments
from a random life on pages that no one will turn to
or care about, and understandably? For I know
the ones that count are not there, nor ever will be,
bound in a private book no one will ever see.

# The Portrait on the Wall

She hung, appropriately he always felt, above
the drinks cabinet in his sitting room. A good deal
older when the artist caught her than he was
when he bought her, that fiery-eyed handsome
woman must have endured many rough days
and Soho drinking nights, modelling, posing
and who knows what else. He could see it in her
face, no longer beautiful but full of character and
a knowing grace. A lady confident of her place.

Night after night, for more years than he'd like
to count, he'd been pouring himself a stiff drink
and holding her in his gaze. She must have been
quite a girl, he always thought. He'd long had an
eye for a good thing, especially where women were
concerned, as they often were, and he'd bought her
in his free-wheeling bachelor days for a song from a
dealer strapped for cash and glad to see her gone.

She never smiled, and he often wondered what
she made of the young man who scrutinised her
with a look she could have taken as lascivious, but
wasn't. Or now, when he could hardly be called young.

She never changed, she never would, enjoying her
settled age, while these decades on his hair had greyed
and lines were tracing their indelible message across
his face. Older now than her, the irony of it would often
make him laugh as he spun some jazz to life on what
she would perhaps have called a phonograph.

He'd be gone before too long, he knew. And she?
Most probably be up for sale again with galleries vying
to hang her in their corridors. But it wouldn't be the same.
Meanwhile he'd put on an upbeat song or two and pour
himself a double of his favourite tipple from a bottle on
the nearby shelf, continuing to drink her health.

# The Stranger

Who is that stranger
on the stair? I've seen
him before but I
can't think where.

He looks me in the eye
and stares and stares.
He seems to be dressed
in clothes I've worn for years.

That song he whistles
is one I often sing,
but it's taken on
a hollow ring.

If I call out to him
he won't respond,
and if I grew bolder
and grabbed at his
shoulder it would
make things worse.

He'd just leave me
with a curse, and I'd become
the stranger on the stair,
banished forever
to I know not where.

# M'Lady

M'Lady has seen them all,
more than she can possibly recall.
Some proudly tall
some small,
some hardly there at all.

In her room they
come, they go, and
they aren't talking
of Michelangelo.

M'Lady never beats
about the bush, with
her secrets discreetly
hidden away, she
always wins the day.

She likes to laugh
and she loves to dance,
but won't for a moment
drop her watchful stance.

Not one for show,
if someone doesn't
make the grade, arrives
too soon, too late, she'll
just up sticks and go.

M'Lord has much to answer for
but she doesn't really care.
She holds all the cards, plays
them with consummate skill,
ever-ready for a tempting thrill.

She's in demand, smartly
clad and *très très chère*,
you wouldn't want to cross
her on a darkened stair.

M'Lady has seen them all.
More than she cares to recall.

# Another Round

That night he took care to leave before
the barman called for last orders, strolling
out into the cold deserted street as rain
crisscrossed the swaying amber lights, his
mood matched by the shifting shadows.

Arriving home he'd fumbled with his key,
managing eventually to slide it into the old
rusty lock he kept on meaning to change.
Clearly he'd drunk a good deal more than
he thought he had. But these empty days
it always seemed to be that way.

Slumping into a chair he clicked the TV
on, but there was nothing there to match
the bonhomie of the company he'd just
left. The company of strangers it might
have been, but they never pried and
they asked no more of him than a few
friendly words and a round or two.

Staggering up the stairs towards his
lonely room he thought of happier times
when he'd shared it with someone he'd
truly loved. This was no way to celebrate
their anniversary. He looked at the photo
that always stood on the table by the
head of his bed, as he did every day.
Would memories of her ever go away?

The next evening, he'd doubtless be back
settling into his usual place beside the bar.
And with any luck the woman in the bright
red dress who'd smiled at him the night
before as he'd moved towards the door
would be there again, and this time he'd
finally summon up the courage to throw her
a surreptitious wink and offer her a drink.

Perhaps she'd bring him the camaraderie
he sought, and maybe, who knows, they'd
leave together, so that when he finally reached
home the walk up those dark winding stairs
would no longer be a lonely one.

He'd drink to that.

# Parting Ways

A large, overweight jovial man with
a long white beard and an even longer
black silk-like coat bulging at the front, he
seemed to have stepped right out of the bible.
His black skull cap appeared glued to his head.
I couldn't hear what it was he said.

But it was from the kerb he'd stepped and
not the scriptures, and into the middle
of a busy main road, everything at sixes
and sevens as he raised his powerful arms
commandingly towards the heavens.

Miraculously, without a curse, without a hoot,
the traffic stopped for him, the drivers of the
normally impatient cars and buses seemingly
transfixed, as I was, hunched behind my wheel.
Somehow it didn't seem at all real.

He could have been Moses parting the Red Sea,
that charismatic man, pursuing Egyptian chariots
racing behind him, but as far I could see no one
was chasing him that ordinary weekday afternoon
and it wasn't the Red Sea, just the Finchley Road
across which he majestically strode.

# Say It in Yiddish

I never learnt that language nor ever will,
and there aren't that many who speak it still.
Yet its fruity words and phrases hang like
lanterns in my head, heard from childhood,
the lingua franca of a lost generation.

Whenever I'm stuck for words, they surface,
uncalled for, half-remembered. Always keep
a *patch* in pocket, my grandfather used to advise,
something up your sleeve. A wise man with no time
for tall stories or braggarts, for *bubbeh meissehs* or
*shvitzers*, he was always direct, often surprisingly
so for such an upright Englishman. Fortunately
much of his colourful *shtik* is lost in translation!

Thus the private lexicon of Yiddish words on which
I drew gradually grew. I learnt that you didn't go bust
but *mechula*, swindlers and thieves were *ganefs*
or *shysters*, a dickhead or fool a *schmuck*, a *shlemiel*,
a bastard was a *momser,* a cheap garment a *shmatta.*

True, *faute de mieux*, phrases and words from other
languages would come to fall readily from this English tongue.
*Angst, wunderkind, zeitgeist, chin chin, faux pas,*
*déjà vu, hasta la vista, ciao, savoir faire, siesta, über...*
*Ooh là là,* an endless list but *je ne regrette rien,*
*auf wiedersehen, vive la difference, c'est magnifique*!

But when you really want to insult someone, whether
a *pisher*, a *shikker*, a *shnorrer*, a *yenta* or a *meshuganer*,
Yiddish takes both the strudel and the bagel.
So *bon apetit*, but mind those false teeth as you
chew, those *falze tsener.* There's no use sighing,
just raise your glass and say *l'chaim*.

# A Locked-Down Chanukah

On that first night of Chanukah my true love lit
with me the first of the eight colourful candles
in our chanukiah, casting a warm glow over the
darkened window. Then she sang with me the
Ma'oz Tzur melody our family had sung together for
as long as we could remember. But this locked-down
year we sang alone, while sensing around us the
presence of departed loved ones and of the young
who'd always enriched our celebrations with the
songs they'd sung and the dreidels they'd spun.

On each of Chanukah's eight nights we lit the
candles, every night an extra one, but it was on
the sixth that my truly alarmed love informed me
we had the company of six large wasps a-buzzing
and staggering round the kitchen as if drunk.
Two were induced to exit safely through a quickly-
opened window, but the other four escaped us,
suddenly dropping as if drugged to the floor.

We paused, we pondered, before picking up
our books again, lighting the six candles and
preparing to sing, my true love upset yet
relieved we had managed to avoid their sting.

On the last day of Chanukah, all the eight
candles alight and standing tall, my true love
and I began to recall the Chanukah story,
the heroic battles of the Maccabees against the
occupying Syrian armies and the miracle of the
cruse of oil that burned for eight days amidst
the ruins of Jerusalem's temple. Then, to our
horror, as we thought back over the years to the
childhood thrill of hearing those stories, not a
partridge, not a turtle dove, not a calling bird,
but a large wood pigeon hit our kitchen window
like a stone, falling to the earth below.

Startled, my true love clung to me dismayed.
She'd become fond of that bird and its three
equally stout companions, its family perhaps,
watching as they waddled up and down the
lawn most days fearlessly, glad of the bread
and bits of cake she always left for them.

We edged towards the door, but stopped,
transfixed, as we caught sight of its crumpled
body, feathers everywhere, and as another
large bird appeared from nowhere, lifting
the dead pigeon in its beak and flying with it
at an astonishing speed across the garden
like a burglar fleeing the scene of his crime.

To bury it perhaps? We hoped as much, our
disturbed thoughts eventually returning to the
interrupted service before my still shaken true love
and I retired to bed, the eight candles burning on
long into a night we'd regret and not readily forget.

# Such Great Times

Come holiday time we'd be off to
France en famille, staying in an elegant
old apartment block facing the sea,
an annual pilgrimage our daughters
looked forward to eagerly.

Every so often, the lift would be 'Hors
Service' and we'd traipse up several flights
of stairs, but we didn't really care. There
were colourful characters everywhere
to talk and laugh about in the flats we passed,
especially a strange, remote man on the first
floor the girls believed was a spy.

But it was the venerable Count Bourg de Bossas
(aka Beaux-Arse) who took the gateau and his
very much younger wife, the Countess, who'd
stand at the edge of the water complaining about
the 'cacas' in the sea and no doubt waiting for him
to pop off so she could grab the booty and flee.

The Count liked to ride of a morning, perhaps
reminding himself of passed glories. But when
his horse was led ceremoniously into the flat's
courtyard, it took three or four willing hands
to help him mount and just as many to get
him down when he eventually rode back in.

Mid-morning he'd arrive on the beach with his
walking stick, stagger into to the sea, then wave
it frantically for someone to heave him out.
Sometimes the honour fell to me. I think he must
have thought the French commanded the sea.

It was like being in the middle of a French farce,
especially when the ladies of a certain age reached
the beach, prattling on about their health and the
state of their bowels as they laid out their towels.
Their husbands must have been swallowed long
ago by the night, for very few had one in sight.

There was the aptly named Madame Bonasse,
and the jovial Madame Bonnet, whose name
made me think of the Latin declensions that
earned me many detentions – bona, bonas, bonet.
I couldn't forget that. And not to be ignored was
the formidable Madame Moutons who lived in the
flats next to ours. Every evening she'd appear on
her balcony with a drink and a tiny dog that never
stopped barking or sleep. Perhaps, given its mistresses'
name, it thought it should be rounding up sheep!

When the ladies entered the sea, it was like
a kind of pageantry, and when they came out
the chatter never stopped, except at 12.30 on the dot
when like a well-trained regiment they turned and
marched in for lunch, leaving us to our baguettes
and the relative silence of the breaking waves.

It was all very different from Southend-on-Sea
where my parents liked to take me.

# When Winds Blow

We need to trim that sky-high sycamore
at the bottom of our garden. Every year
it looks down on us ever more threateningly,
but it has a grandeur that makes us hesitate
even though we know that if it fell its great trunk
would shatter the roof of our house.

Deceptively, on calm summer days, as the sun illuminates
its branches and we marvel at its majestic beauty,
it appears far too sturdy and innocent for that.

Yet when the wind rages and those whipped branches
bend and bow like courtiers from side to side, it looks
as if they'll bring it crashing down. But they don't,
and somehow it continues both to survive and thrive.
Its leaves too are always the last to concede.

It must be every bit as old as me, that tall proud tree,
and sometimes I tell myself I must try to emulate it
as the years grow alarmingly high, as life's treacherous
winds take hold unexpectedly and I too begin to sway.

For my part I'll be doing all I can to stay as I am, bending
and swaying, determined to avoid any kind of trimming
however dangerously the winds rise, hoping to avoid
a surgeon of any kind, tree or otherwise.

# A Silent Toast

We know each other as well as two
people can, have shared exultant moments
of birth and celebration, a lifetime almost,
the low moments too, of loss and desolation.

And yet tonight, across a wooden kitchen
table, sharing a simple meal, you seem
distraught. What thoughts are troubling you,
I wonder, as you look forlornly towards me.
I ought to know but clearly don't.
That can't be right.

Rain is rattling the windows, the night is
darker than dark. I'd like to raise my hand
like a skilled magician and vanish them, whatever
the demons be, but am unable to.

Your hair, longer than usual, rests on your
shoulders as it used to do, and as I raise my
eyes I see the beautiful woman I've shared
the years with come into view.

Who, I wonder, do you see?
A distant man, deep in his own thoughts,
perhaps, almost a stranger, if only momentarily.

Silence pulsates round the room expectantly.
The glasses of wine I'd poured remain untouched.

And then, like a plane emerging from the clouds,
like a flash of sunlight, you smile, and I smile back,
relieved, those healing smiles more potent
than any reassuring words could ever be.

Our hands reach towards each other simultaneously.
We raise and clink our glasses in a silent toast.

# For the Record

They've been piling up in the cupboard
under the stairs for years, those old diaries,
like there's no tomorrow, and who can
say whether there will be. Yet I can never
bring myself to throw them away,

though there's nothing of interest in
them, even to me: random dates for lunches
and dinners, car services, holidays, unwelcome
appointments with doctors and dentists becoming
more frequent as the years advanced.

Even the social invitations appear less engaging
than in the carefree early days, hot dates that
have long since cooled. Memory recalls far more
colourful encounters than those the scribble on
the crumpled pages records. The fading covers
too lack variety – dull reds and blues, easy to confuse.

I've long relished the gossipy diaries of history, of
Pepys, the Goncourt brothers, Chips Channon and all
the others, but mostly they were written for publication,
for strangers to read, which allowed their sharp pens all
kinds of mischievous liberties, while my old shabby
diaries just told me where to turn up and when.

Next year I'll burn the lot... or maybe not.

# Change of Address

Nothing would be the same. We'd left,
everything packed away. The books, many
old, their pages curled, recalled a vanished world.
Only the shelf-lined walls remained.

What joyous times we had there, celebrations, song.
Sadder moments too, and intimate ones
when the piano was closed, the guests gone!

Hard to imagine others roaming round rooms
that had our hallmark, furniture we'd chosen with care,
paintings neatly spaced between the shelves,
and here and there the bric-a-brac we didn't
really need, mostly bought on holidays abroad
at prices we could ill-afford.

Perhaps if we dropped by we'd be let in to see
the changes within, but however extreme, the
walls would remain much as they'd always been,

maybe a crack or two here and there, easy
to repair, and when those occupants in turn
moved on, as move on, in time, they would,

there'd be all-change again, fresh paint, furniture,
things we'd left behind dispersed, shelves now gone,
while those walls, their solid selves, looked on.

As for the garden, would it still be staring
through the sitting-room windows, wondering
where we'd gone, the flowers round the lawn forlorn.

Hardly so, for we've come to know that wherever
you go, wherever you roam, everything you think
you own you only have on loan.

# Behind the Screen

The urgent ping of my mobile and a flash of light
took me unawares that early January morning
as I slowly emerged from the darkness of sleep
and night dissolved. Reaching out I grabbed the
phone and tapped the code in mindlessly. Hard
to ignore: you never knew what might lurk
behind that passive screen, waiting to be seen.

That cold winter morning the usual bargain offers
flowed, but an arresting news item roused me from
my reverie. There, online, was a newly discovered
archive of photos from Occupied France. Despite
my apprehension I felt compelled to view them.

Charming at first, disarming photos of carefree
children playing in the countryside unrolled, their
parents watching lovingly. The sun shone. There
seemed to be jollity everywhere. Then, as if from
nowhere, a lengthening shadow appeared and
that earlier idyllic scene suddenly disappeared.

Filling the screen now, and following each other in
swift succession, were ever more horrific close-up
photos of laughing Nazi soldiers brutally forcing
those same children to line up alongside a cluster
of fern trees, and the adults too, before gunning them
down as callously as they could until no one stood.

So immediate those scenes you could practically
hear the screams and then, almost louder, a silence
as the unflinching camera lens moved steadily in,
this time on piles of bones and skeletal heads piled
high as if from an obscene bonfire, with yet more
soldiers cheering a job well done.
A curse on them.

Who was the photographer? How could he focus
so steadily? And whose bones were they?
Fathers, mothers, children? The old, the frail?
Impossible to identify, to believe these
bones once lived, celebrated, laughed, played,
perhaps even that they prayed.

I switched to off, but the images wouldn't fade,
stayed with me the whole day and the ensuing
night, and for days and nights to come.
A vision of hell I couldn't dispel.

Photos from long ago they might have been,
but as real to me as if taken the other week
in a nearby street. Never will I forget,
and never can I forgive, having as I do
the privilege to live.

# A New Love

She hopped towards me fearlessly
as, kneeling, I slowly turned over the
hard earth, my annual task, an old
wheelbarrow full of carefully chosen
summer plants waiting my attention.

She came so close, that tiny baby
robin, I felt I could easily reach out
and touch her but checked myself,
fearing she would fly were I to try.

Her heart was beating quickly.
Was it love, I wondered? And why did
I assume she was a she, simply because
she'd moved so near to me?

'Take care little friend', I heard myself
whispering, there are cats and hungry
foxes on the hunt round here.

I watched awhile, then placed some
crumbs on my hand and stretched it
gently towards her. She pecked at them
as readily as if they'd been the finest caviar
then darted away on her matchstick legs.

'She's so pretty', my wife declared,
inadvertently interrupting our tryst.
She was indeed, and those unexpected
moments of intimacy we'd shared that
May morning were a special kind of gift
I would not want to have missed.

# All Those Ties

'I thought you were a man without ties'
my best friend's father would quip
whenever I turned up of a weekend
sporting a florid new one.

Many still hang dutifully at the back of a tall
dusty cupboard, brazenly wide or skeleton thin
as the current fashion decreed.

Hard now to imagine them turning the head
of any girl I might then have fancied, yet
week after week I'd squander my precious
pocket money hopefully.

Now, of course, it's cooler not to wear
a tie, though I still do so in my old-fashioned
way when the occasion seems to call for it.
But not one of these, not for the life of me,
though they still hang there invitingly.

One day, I tell myself, I must take them
to the local charity shop, but who would want them?
Besides they're part of me, what I once was,
as many carefully posed photos testify.

So they'll go on hanging there, I suppose,
until I move on, and then they too won't have a say
in whatever fate may come their way.

For myself, I wouldn't be seen dead in any of them.

# Change of Tune

*Willow Weep for Me*, a classic sung movingly
by Billie Holiday and many other great performers
over the years, and one I often hum.

But now, I tell myself, it should be the reverse,
with *us* weeping for the large willow that hangs
forlornly at the garden's edge. Not a leaf
to be seen, not a sign of life, just twisted skeletal
branches stretching pathetically in all directions.

And every night, the same large grey silent bird
settled on them eerily like something out of
a Hitchcock film, as if in mourning. Waiting.

We should, I suppose, have the dead tree
cut down, but my optimistic wife protested.
'Maybe next year it will revive,' she pleaded.
'You never know...'

Unable, as ever, to believe in resurrection
I demurred, if quietly. As she said, you never know...
but that was as far as I was prepared to go.

# The Magic Cup

There's magic in that special silver cup
the young girl says, and in a way she's right,
though not in quite the way she thinks.

When she picks it up, it is with awe, as if
she's drawing King Arthur's legendary
Excalibur itself from its solid bed of stone.
During celebrations it's always centre stage,
and on festivals too as we turn the page.

It certainly has a powerful presence,
but the inscription is what's special for me
going back four generations of our family,
a gift on the wedding of someone dear to
all of us and now long gone. Whenever
I pass by the shelf on which it stands I
find myself pausing as it draws my eye.

Solid, beautifully crafted and more a goblet
than a cup, it's fit for a king or even a prophet
to drink from. Sometimes I think that if I fill it
and make a wish that wish will be fulfilled,
though I know how fanciful that really is.

Still perhaps, as that young girl, our grandchild,
believes, there is indeed some magic in that cup,
of sorts anyway, and I'd like her to be right.

I would never want to be the one to break
the spell it seems to cast. For if nothing else
it remains for me a kind of talisman, reminding
me of my roots, the mystery, the history,
as it will eventually be for her too perhaps
to pass in her turn, in time, along the line.

# Hello, Goodbye

Set out like that it seems so matter of fact, so cold,
two lives from A–Z on two frail certificates each, birth
and death – Hello, Goodbye – and nothing in between.

I take them carefully from the oval, coffin-like box
someone has placed them in, and which it has fallen
to me to sort and care for. I look at the names, not just
of my parents but of witnesses too, my grandparents,
one I hardly knew. But what of the years in between, I
ask myself, thinking of the smiling couple in the wedding
photos I have in another box, that beautiful, happy young
woman, that handsome man, with a whole life before them.

Such hopes, such rich lives, some of which I shared
as I grew towards them, the struggles, the hard work,
the war they survived, all those devoted patients my
father cured, the songs she sang as he accompanied her,
the parties, the laughter, the family gatherings.

Hello, Goodbye. It made me want to cry.

# Calling the Tune

The songs that crowd my head
are there to stay. Whatever I do,
whatever I say, I can't will them away.

Some are children's jingles from
a half-remembered childhood,
mostly in English, a few in French.

Many are from teenage years,
danced to in dimly lit rooms where
Glen Miller and Sinatra held sway,
numbers I still tap my foot to today.

Others have a more commanding note I
can't escape as ancient hymns and psalms
rule the day, and distant choirs have their say.

The chords, it seems, grow richer and
more complex as the years unfold, as
Schubert sonatas and Beethoven quartets
vie with the earlier syncopated numbers.

Yet chords can become discordant,
especially when winter nights impinge
and lamplights sway in the howling wind,
making you feel you've somehow sinned.

But I don't despair, as the blues of Billie
Holiday fill the air and thoughts of Don
Giovanni's romantic tally help me rally.

So play on, I say, and keep those tunes, with
their varied tones and harmonies revolving
in my head, ruling my changing moods for
as long as they will, and I can hum them still.

# Solo Performance

It begins and ends with a solo performance
no one can understudy or double for, one
greeted by cheers, the other laced with tears.

In between you achieve what you can
love, work, study, play, make the most of every day,
or so you should, for you only get one go on life's
precarious merry-go-round as it turns at an
ever quicker pace before its lights flicker, it slows
gradually to a halt, and only an Exit sign glows.

# Not Quite Clear

How strange the voices that come
from seasons past, singing tunes
you've somehow heard before.
And how familiar the shadowy faces
that vie to catch your eye, almost
within reach, not quite in view.

Today I vowed to turn them all away,
to start anew, but what songs now
will echo in the night, and who, if anyone,
will hover in the wings? The seasons
seem to change their fragile scenery with
alarming speed, and lines, like railway
lines, return to whence they came.

It's not a game, this game we're forced
to play, and yet we try to keep the ball
in play as best we can, stall, introduce
what ploys we still can muster, smile.
For the rules are not our rules
and we serve an unknown master.

Here they come again, those unclear
faces, voices, memories, and this time
around I'll welcome them like the friends
they are, relieved to have them with me
as night transcends and I contemplate
a sky pierced by one solitary star,
so near it seems, yet far too far.

# Inside Out

Inside out
and upside down,
I seem to be
living the life
of a clown.

Often too
all's in reverse,
I feel I'm under
some kind of curse.
It's quite perverse.

I shuffle the cards
as best I can,
do my best to get
things straight,
toss and turn and
lie awake, greet
the morning in a
dishevelled state.

I seem to be heading
for the buffers at an
alarming rate. Must
slam my foot down
on the brake...

or leave it in
the hands of fickle
fate to dictate.

# Loud and Clear

*remembering Douglas Hill*


I never discovered how it happened.
Were you day-dreaming, your head full
of the next never-to-be-written poem
or sci fi story, or did that bus driver
just not see you crossing and hit
the brakes too late. Such intelligence
and sensitivity gone in a flash.

In my head I hear those screeching brakes,
the ambulances shrill alarm. I still don't
know where or exactly when, just a
message on our phone from someone
saying they thought we'd want to know.
They couldn't imagine how low the blow.

Steeped in your fulsome letters as I am
today after many lost years, I find myself in
a strange communion with a spirit now long dead.
Or is it that spirits never die?
Author of a book on the Supernatural
you'd have had an answer to that!

As if for the first time, I re-read
your pertinent criticism of the early
poems I'd rashly sent you and those of
yours you'd sent me in return. How
right you were! But always yours is a
warm encouraging voice calling for more.
True friendship thrives on honesty
and there are things one can't ignore.
I loved the gossip too, of course, in letters
from your native Canada where you'd gone
to research a book, soon to return to a

welcoming London you'd made your home.
Also the memories of the time we'd shared
an office, editing other people's books.
You gave me the job and showed me how,
a masterclass that steers me even now.

For our wedding you sent us a fragile Hans
Coper pot, and a poem to accompany it. That
valuable pot fell one cruel day, but the words
remain, just as in these lengthy letters they do,
and in the sci fi books that made your name.

Dear friend, I owe you this, and so much more.
I only wish I could say 'encore'.

# Life Lines

Moving quickly, I fished the struggling
wasp from the water and saved its life.
It lay for a moment on the side, no
doubt gathering its strength, then
took off and began to circle me.

It drew ever closer, threateningly,
then stung my defending arm.
Must be a moral there, I
thought, as I began to swear.

Soon after a grasshopper that had
been watching hopped in for a dip.
But it too couldn't swim. In pain
though I was I did the decent thing,
but it hopped right back in.

At least it didn't sting.

## Advice to Oneself

You can't just spend the rest
of your life waiting for that greatest
of honours, a *Times* Obituary, or
be checking the paper every day
to see if you're there.

Probably only get an inch or two
anyway, if you're lucky, so nothing
to boast about (if boast one could!).

Same with their birthday list,
never mentioned, I'm glad to say.
Who needs that, the whole world
knowing you're well passed your peak?
Not something to which others would
readily turn the other cheek.

What's more the ladies wouldn't
come calling any more, not that they do,
not that they did. So best to get on with it,
and take what comes, just making sure you're
not there when they beat the drums.

# Poet's Corner

Last night as thunder shook, lightning
seared the earth, and a screeching wind
thrashed the trees, haunting scenes
from Macbeth swamped my reeling mind –
the witches on the moor, their strange
curses and death-laden prophesies.

Shaken I sprang from my restless bed,
those chants and unsettling images swirling
round my head, taunting voices urging me
to compose final words to be chiselled on
my own cold stone, when, like a puppet,
I finally kick the proverbial bucket...
tomorrow, or tomorrow, or tomorrow.

It was dark, lighting continued to spit, and
those raucous, bubbling voices spelled
nothing but trouble and wouldn't desist.

Best give them the ghoulish words they crave
I told myself, toss some letters in the air, my
final decree, there for eternity, large, in caps,
black as those cold howling nights on the moor,
rebuffing the wind, the rain, not holy writ
just two stark words catching my fragile mood,
   staring, declaring
      'FUCK IT'.

# Acknowledgements

The encouragement and enthusiasm of a number of people have helped to keep me sane and writing during the dark Covid days. First and foremost my wife Carole, the touchstone on whose good taste and judgement I always rely; our twin daughters, Deborah and Manuela, who guarded us during lockdown and always respond when the vagaries of our capricious computer defeat me; our grandchildren, Lauren, Sam and Caitlin, whose various talents and enthusiasms made us look to a rosy future when we were obsessed with the frightening present.

Maureen Lipman encouraged me to pick up my pen again after some 40 years as a publisher had sapped my poetic juices, read my new poems with me at various literary festivals and events, and always responds to any new poems I send her with the kind of warmth and understanding that would keep any poet writing. Sally Dunsmore, Director of the Oxford Literary Festival, has proved a true friend, regularly inviting me to read at her fabulous festival, as has Claudia Rubenstein, Director of Jewish Book Week. Stephen Pollard, when editor of the JC, published a number of my poems; others have appeared in the *Camden New Journal*, *Acumen*, *WLS Review* and *Jewish Renaissance*. I've also been lucky to have shared a stage at recent events with two peerless singers, Norma Winstone and Jacqui Dankworth, as well as with such outstanding musicians as Art Themen, Christian Garrick, Charlie Wood and Dave Green.

I'm grateful to Caroline Bloom for the family's silver goblet that inspired my poem; to David Abse for the special picture he painted at his atelier in France for the cover of this book (thus continuing a precious link with the Abse family and his parents, Joan and Dannie); to Chris Beetles for generously offering to host the launch for this book at his superb gallery in Ryder Street; to my old friends Anthony Harkavy, whose sharp lawyer's eyes never miss a slip, and Edward Gold, who helped me organise the very first poetry and jazz concert at the old Hampstead Town Hall back in the swinging sixties; to Sandra Parsons, Susie Dowdall and Bel Mooney, always supportive; to writers Eilat and Yehuda Koren, whose warm voices regularly call out to me from Jerusalem, and Elizabeth Davies (Rose), Robson Books' incomparable first editor who continues to offer me sage suggestions whenever I send her poems. I'm also grateful to Rabbi David Mitchell for making me the unofficial Poet Laureate of WLS (doubtless the only honour I will ever receive), and for the continued encouragement of Peter Brookes and Alfred Brendel, both of whom I was privileged to publish.

Finally, a big hand for Laurie De Decker, the meticulous gem of an editor who picked up my careless mistypings and helped me prepare the manuscript of this book in the format required by my publisher.